ESP

Eric Stephen Peffley

ESP

COPYRIGHT © 2020 BY ERIC STEPHEN PEFFLEY / CASA DE PEFFLEY, INC.

ALL RIGHTS RESERVED. PRINTED IN THE UNITED STATES OF AMERICA. NO PART OF THIS BOOK MAY BE USED OR REPRODUCED, DISTRIBUTED OR TRANSMITTED IN ANY MANNER OR BY ANY MEANS WHATSOEVER, WITHOUT PRIOR WRITTEN PERMISSION.

FOR MORE INFORMATION, PLEASE CONTACT PEFFLEYERIC@GMAIL.COM

THE AUTHOR GRATEFULLY ACKNOWLEDGES ALL WHO WERE A SOURCE OF INSPIRATION FOR THE WORKS CONTAINED WITHIN THIS BOOK.

ALL ORIGINAL ILLUSTRATIONS BY ERIC STEPHEN PEFFLEY

PEFFLEY, ERIC STEPHEN / CASA DE PEFFLEY, INC. / QUESTION SHIT MEDIA
A JENERIC PRODUCTION

LOS ANGELES, CALIFORINA 90046
DESIGNED BY JENNA OHNEMUS PEFFLEY

ESP 2020 /PEFFLEY, ERIC STEPHEN
ISBN 978-0-578-66856-7

FIRST EDITION

for Sandy and Steve
with gratitude every day

*I kid
you some,*

but

*I shit
you none.*

TABLE OF CONTENTS

ON THY WAY ... 9

DIVE BAR ANGEL ... 10

THE DAY SOCIAL MEDIA WENT DOWN FOR A FEW MINUTES ... 12

PLASTIC IDOL ... 13

POETRY FOR BEGINNERS ... 14

THE MOAN RANGER ... 16

E. PLURIBUS DENIM ... 18

NEW YEAR'S MORNING WALK OF SHAME ... 20

PARTY IN THE HEARTLAND ... 22

JESUS RODE A JACKASS ... 24

MANIFESTATION OF A SHOULDER DEVIL ... 28

SUNSHINE ON A STICK ... 30

CAP'N ... 32

SHANTI CAKE ... 34

LITTLE BUSKER GIRL ... 35

BALLAD OF THE SODIE WATER UNICORN ... 36

NOSTALGIA (PART 1) ... 37

DON OBLOQUY ... 38

CONSERVATIVE CRACKER ... 41

COGITARE ET SENTIRE ... 42

HINDSIGHT IS BUT(T) A SPHINCTER ... 44

QUESTION SHIT ... 47

PAM ... 50

BUSTA' ... 51

MIRROR ... 52

TABLE OF CONTENTS

CHINESE FOOD	53
SHIPMATES	54
TALL TALE FROM A SHALLOW GUTTER	56
TOO STONED TO SLOW DANCE	59
ONE MONTH CHIP	60
EVER	62
"JAM UP!"	63
THE ALGORITHM OF "IZ"	64
MASON JAR MEMORIES	67
MOTHER MOLLOY	68
MY DOG IS NOT A CAT PERSON	71
A WIFE'S LAMENT	72
THE DILETTANTE AND THE RENAISSANCE MAN	73
THEM!	74
EXPRESSION OF GOD	75
PRESSURE	76
OUTPOURING OF LIKE	77
EUROPE PLAYLIST	78
ASSPOCI LA BUTTE	80
PARLE VOUS JE'TAIME	83
THE TAO OF GRANDPA ROMAN	84
SELF LOVE	85
NOSTALGIA (PART 2)	86
PICTURE OF THREE	88
WE	93

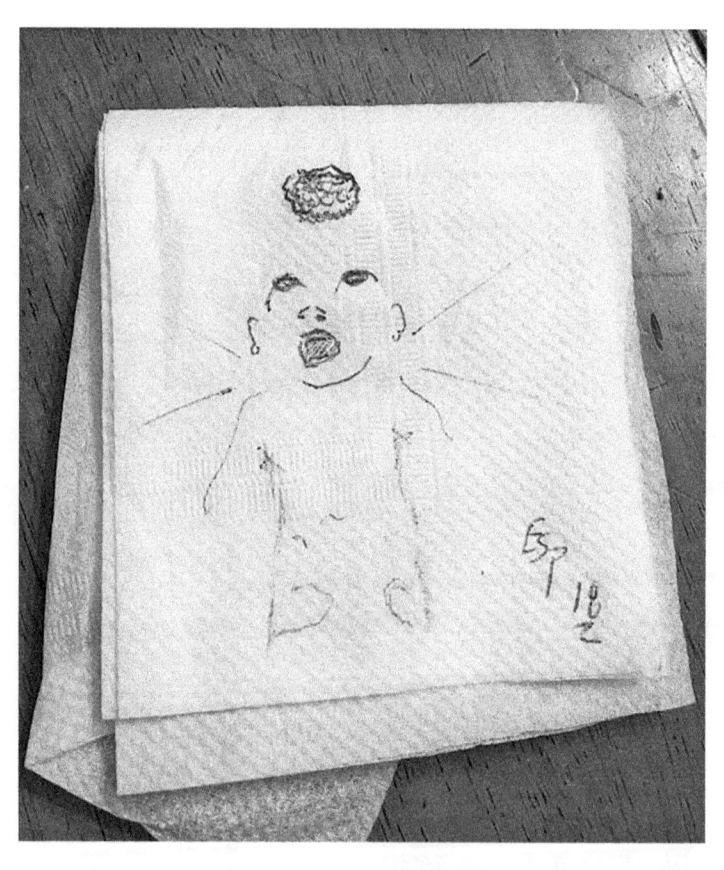

ON THY WAY

to
wa
rd
the
ne
xt
fi
as
co
go
wi
th
God.

DIVE BAR ANGEL

Won't you pick me up
And dust me off
Shine my last dirty glass,
Relieve this tired cough
I'm too blind to drive
My legs can't stand to walk
Back to the outskirts of heaven

Baby blue denim rusting
Shadow's split for the night
Mis amigos me han dejado
To the serpent knife fight
Her hand reaches toward me
But something's not right
High noon at a half past eleven

Dive bar angel
Won't you take me to bed
Dive bar angel
Place your wreath round my head
Dive bar angel
Lie to me,
    say I'm not dead

Dive Bar Angel…

Sweet nothings whispered
Hard lessons learned
Whippoorwill whistle
Train coal as it burns

Dive bar angel
Please take me to bed
Dive bar angel
Place one final kiss
upon my forehead
Dive bar angel
It's not like in all the
    books that I've read

Dive Bar Angel...

THE DAY SOCIAL MEDIA WENT DOWN FOR A FEW MINUTES

May the cold long lonely disconnected night
give way to new and better days of old:
Children playing kickball in the street,
Postcoital lovers cast in the ember glow of cigarettes burning
in place of isolating blue smartphone screens,
Our likes, once again, so simple as a smile, so sure as a nod...
hold up, facebook's coming back online •

PLASTIC IDOL

We need plastic bags
To carry plastic rings
That hold the plastic bottles
We pour into plastic cups

For we the plastic people
To drink through plastic straws
While clutching plastic sporks
To shovel plastic food

Off of plastic plates
Into peckish plastic mouths
Past perfect plastic teeth
Down polished plastic bowels

On to the plastic ocean
Under placid plastic sky
Beneath a plastic heaven
And our god made out of plastic!

POETRY FOR BEGINNERS

some poems
are like
whoopee cushions

be careful where you sit

while

other poems
are like
makin' whoopee

be careful not to shit where you eat

while

other poems
are like
whoopie pies

mmm, mmmmm, mmmmmmm,
now that's a tasty poem

while still

other poems
are like
the nineteen-ninety-five
Whoopi Goldberg
star vehicle "Theodore Rex"

and this
is one
of those poems—

be careful!

THE MOAN RANGER

Why oh why
do I waste all of my data
on the LTE?
    and
Why oh why
buy the cow
when i could just have
the milk for free?

My oh my, all these whys
are surely gonna be the death of me

Help me, Ke-mo Sah-bee!
Ke-mo Sah-bee, won't you please help me?

Shoofly pie is mighty yummy
but it rots away your gums and teeth
Gettin' high is mostly funny
'till you get in dutch with the police

I'd ask her out
but I'm too darn shy
Won't wipe my derrière
because it's single ply
I'm too content to itch,
and bitch, & moan & sigh
Always askin' "why?"

Why oh why
did the mob chase the monster
up into a tree?
    and
Why oh why

must a clown be made to wallow
in his misery?

Me oh my, there must be more
to this story that I just can't see

Tell me, Ke-mo Sah-bee!
Ke-mo Sah-bee, please enlighten me.

I oughta cry but I'm afraid
emotional release will cause me
too much grief
When the priest said,
"Go in peace."
I knew his words would bring
no real relief

She was the wormy Apple
of my eye
Could've been a contender
if I'd only tried
'Was too content to kvetch,
and bitch, & moan & sigh
Charlie, why oh why?

blame the other guy…

                                          french fucking fry.

E PLURIBUS DENIM

Got a pair
I like to wear
A second skin
To hang out in
That shade of blue
My favorite hue
A flag to fly
High when I die

Pearly buttons
On my shirt
Feet of sand
And hands of dirt
Collar open
Toward the sky
A blanket under
Stars to lie

Friend to every
Creed & stripe
Ballpoint pen
And pocket knife
Workman's armor
Leisure style
Keep it simple
With a smile

From Californ'
To Place LaRue
Canadian
Tuxedo true
Cowboy sinner
Saloon stool saint
Paired with necktie
Sure as shit ain't

"Out of many, denim"
Far and wide
For the lonesome
Long abide
Cotton heaven
Worn with pride
Fabric poem
Testified

NEW YEAR'S MORNING WALK OF SHAME

may last night's acquaintance
be forgot, and never brought to…
(pukes outside of Uber)
dear God please don't let
her/me be pregnant
(shiver)
I swear I'll wear a coat
next time ~

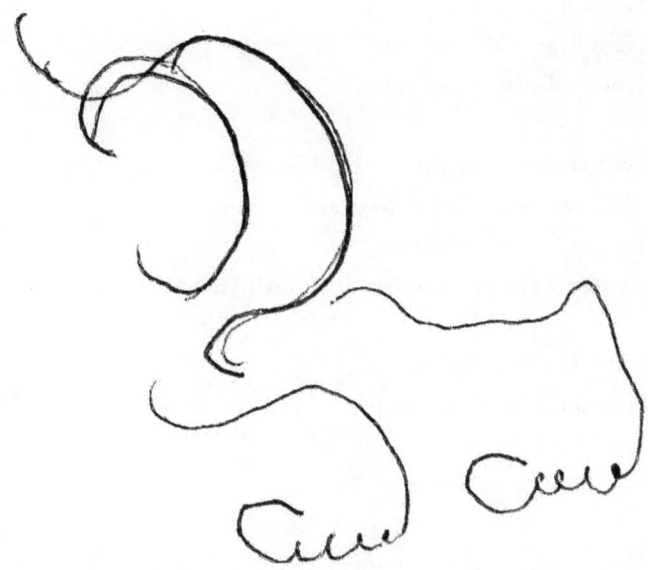

PARTY IN THE HEARTLAND

I may be dirt poor
But I'm c'untry to the core
Bought a boat / It won't float
'Cause I filled it full of buckshot /
Slam a shot of gut-rot!

Flag high / Semper Fi
Pray to God on Sunday
Truck load / Back road
You know it's just another Monday

Boots on / Doggone
Gotta make it over hump day
Neon sign / Moonshine
Double fistin' on a Friday

And Hank Jr. sangin'
"All my rowdy friends have settled down"
But take a look around
At all my rowdy friends still throwin' down

Shit Howdy! / Tell me
How'd he, how'd he do that?
Yee-haw / Sawed off
Giddy-up now lets go!

(Insert lame-ass guitar solo here)

I'm a Redneck
But I'm proud as heck
White hat / Blue jeans
Life is just a one night keg stand /
Another party in the Heartland

Beer goggles / bobber wobbles
Think I got one on the line
She ain't no "10" but I ain't neither
Baby, maybe we can pass the time /
Pretty darlin' pass the wine

(Yeah, now we're gettin' loose—
Straight mommy juice to that caboose!)

Shit Howdy!
Y'all that's just the way we do it
Yee-haw / Sawed off
Giddy-up now let's go!

JESUS RODE A JACKASS
(Inspired by John Prine, & Billy Joe Shaver by way of Kinky Friedman)

Jesus laid a dusty Navajo blanket
across the back of a braying donkey
Saddled up to head out West
to meet the world
Saying, "One fish should be just plenty,
with all this bread that is my body…"
He untied his man-bun,
and down his hair unfurled

"Goodbye!" cried Mother Mary,
"Take this rosary to remember me."
Jesus kissed her so long
and hung it 'round his neck
Then Joseph handed him a cross that he
had whittled from an Apple tree
"When your back's against it, son,
be sure to give 'em heck."

Jesus rode in on a jackass
blood alcohol content
of one hundred percent
The law was not sure whence he came
or where he went
Jesus rode atop a jackass
Decanter made flesh
of fermented sacrament
The sinners all agreed
he must have been Heaven sent

Jesus rode in on a jackass
so those Megachurch charlatans
might somehow repent
"How could they prey on those
who can barely pay their rent?"
Jesus rode atop a jackass
but the money machine
would simply not relent
Phony prophets, for profits only,
were hell-bent

Jesus was thinking about giving up
and building him an Earthship in Taos
When he felt his mama
hangin' there next to his heart
And pulling his adoptive father's unadorned cross
from a leather pouch
He thought, "Heck, pop,
why, this is only the start."

So after three days rest up in a cave somewhere,
good ol' reliable Jesus was at it again
This time more committed
than before
Fearing not sword, spear, bullet, bomb,
nor otherwise the tyranny of evil men
Armed only with love, Jesus was ready
to even the score

Jesus rode in on a jackass
to LA by way of Damascus
making friends and
sharing laughter along the way
Jesus rode atop a jackass
fixin' to start a little fracas
as he prayed to help to make
a brighter day ~

MANIFESTATION OF A SHOULDER DEVIL
(me and Mr. B)

A silver maned
Shakespeare reciting
Beanery haunting
Shoulder devil
Said he hailed from Pittsburg
Around the time of the '68 riots
And the drinks were on him

Six foot eleven if he was an inch!
That som'bitch...

Oh
What the hell?
We can always climb back on the wagon
Tomorrow,
and   tomorrow,
and   tomorrow...

Today's for hangin' out
and hangin' on
Givin' in
and gettin' gone
Idiot tales
and bottomless ales
Tequila neats
Down bourbon streets—
and
            Away!

Away,

down Gower Avenue,
With a Rainbow in the rear view,
Past the old Pioneer Chicken—
Away...

A way out where the road dead ends:
    PIONEER TOWN
  (with a billion stars all around)

For one final round
Of J Tree tattooed Del Taco
Troubadour dreams
of Greenblatt's #7
in Room #8

Hungover again.
With the ghost of Gram's chorus
Faintly calling us home

From...

The Twilight Zone.

SUNSHINE ON A STICK

She's sunshine on a stick!
The sweetest citrus
This side of Sunset Boulevard

Plump hips on a toothpick
A pulpy mistress
Of the Hollywood avant-garde

And all those Vitamin C deficient idols
Of silver screen and crummy commercials
Secretly wish they could be
"In Like Flynn"
To bag the bombshell Marilyn

Before her smile goes out of season
And the next
Farmer's Market Fashion
Comes along.

CAP'N

Captain of his Chrysler
Steadfast Stegosaurus
Fossil of Fountain Avenue
Rover of the asphalt forest

Almost had a bit part once
upon a smog-choked time
But his boat won't
pass emissions now
that he can see the city skyline

Just a crusty, carefree
could-have-been
With a shotgun ridin' Gilligan
The parts aren't his to lose or win
His role is "pass the wine"

A could-not-care-less with a grin
Move over, Little Buddy,
the reviews are in:
Critics all agree, the story's pretty thin
The plot is pay no mind

Captain of his K-Car
Dilapidated Dinosaurus
Leftover on Las Palmas
Forty years a tourist

They said he'd end up face down in a gutter!
Well, it hasn't been for lack of tryin'...
They said he couldn't get arrested in this town!
Though he sure could commit the crimes ~

SHANTI CAKE
(for Tanner)

Shanti Cake
Piece of the pie
Song of the soul
Tear in the eye

Smile on my lips
Rhyme on my tongue
Burden laid down
Sweet praises sung

Shanti Cake
Peace if we try
No River so deep
Nor Mountain as high

Still stands the ladder
Calm every rung
One step at a time
The heartstring is strung

Shanti Cake
Peace by and by
Songs softly hush
Tears shed and dry

In silence golden
Now counted among
Those holy anointed
And forever young

LITTLE BUSKER GIRL
(for Torie)

Busk me a song, ye gym cowgirl
Be thine my muse between arm curls
Workout music don't usually move me
Unless played by a cowgirl so groovy

Busk me a ditty, gym gypsy
I'm benching the bar plus a 50
And standard jock jams
Never steady my hands
Like the street serenade of a hippie

O,
Busk me a tune, ye gym lady
Keep me motivated
Not lazy
The Sweat Life is sweet
But it's never complete
Without your melody
For which I am
Crazy

BALLAD OF THE SODIE WATER UNICORN

I'm a sodie water unicorn
I got sparkling water for my horn
I don't drink no liquor made of corn
Not no more

I'm a sodie water unicorn
But I'm not forlorn
In fact I'm feeling reborn

Unicorn! UNICORN!

bubble, bubble, fizzzzzzz, clomp
bubble, bubble, clomp
bubble, bubble, fizzzzzzz, clomp
bubble, bubble, clomp

I'm a sodie water unicorn
I slowly shed my Viking drinking horn
I no longer bare the crown of thorns
I once bore

Just a reformed loadie unicorn
Feeling no scorn
Mineral water adorned

Unicorn! UNICORN!

fizzzzzzz, bubble, bubble, clomp
fizzzzzzz, bubble, bubble
fizzzzzzz, bubble, bubble, clomp
fizzzzzzz, clomp, clomp

NOSTALGIA (PART 1)

There was a guy when we were kids
that gave out nose kazoos one Halloween
with the promise of a FULL-SIZE candy bar
the following year to any One Of Us
who came back and could blow him a tune.
Union Deposit Legend has it
that our friend Darcie's older brother
did in fact go on to master that thing
and collect his bounty.

He has since passed away,
and who knows what ever became of the kazoo guy,
but it's memories such as these
of the tiny glories of youth
that I sometimes
in my quieter moments
find almost
overwhelmingly
moving.

DON OBLOQUY

bloviating feckless ass
atop an elephant does ride
bulbous frame
protruding mass
perturbing patter
inanely crass
"To the windmills!"
on he raves
"Lock her up!"
he chants for days
and just for fun, to pass the time,
a handicapp-ed pantomime
for the web trolls wild delight
he feigns coherence through the night
no loyal Sancho for his squire
he'll build a wall with razor wire
"Oh, Stormy Dulcinea, wait—
While I make this country great!"
red bedpan his helmet snug
french fry saber raised to plug
his pursing lips before he shouts,
"Charge!" out of his fast food mouth
and on he lumbers toward the mill
a windy phantom foe to kill
before it can supply the juice
for cable news to cook his goose

"I hope that when the feed goes down,
my Fox and Friends are still around…"
and even though this makes no sense
politely nodding, there sits Pence
waiting for his Mother Dear
who is his wife,
now ain't that queer?
as Cheeto's tossed by mighty blade
birds wing by, oddly unscathed
and just as Donnie's chips seem down
a bareback Russkie bot a-bounds
into the frey, the juggernaut
as Mueller shrugs,
"T'was all for naught"
    A MIGHTY TUSSLE
       KICKS UP DUST
the victor's fate

    IN GOD WE TRUST.

CONSERVATIVE CRACKER

I'm a conservative cracker
I chews my chewin' tobaccer
Confederate flag on my tractor
Don't tread on me
Boots for shit-kickin'
Camo pants so I blend in
With the rest of my white kin
Freedom ain't free

Lazy freeloaders
Crossin' our borders
Libtard sports players
Taking a knee
Better take cover
Like snowflakes in summer
literal mother fucker
Proud S.O.B.

And I am my own daddy
I pledge allegiances gladly
So all you cuck-suckers
Can go 'head and pucker
And kiss me right 'tween the cheeks

(Ass cheeks that is.
That don't make me gay do it?
Act'ully, that feels kinda guhd...)

"Oh say does that Star Spangled
 Banner yet wave
 O'er the land of the free
 And the home of the Craven"

COGITARE ET SENTIRE

"I hate, therefore I am!"
"I am, therefore I hate!"
This is the mantra by which
I will make this country great

"I am, therefore I hate!"
"I hate, therefore I am!"
I will take this country back
    (Way Back!)
And make it goddamn great again!

We fear what we don't know
We know not what we fear
But insight is for losers
While a winner's path is clear

We know not what we fear
We fear what we don't know
Where jackboots went a-marching
That's where we are bound to go

Where red hats now go marching
So too shall we blindly follow?

We must learn from the past
This much may very well be true
But history repeats itself so often
That it's seldom something new

"Forgive them," it once was said
"for they know not what they do."
If Christ upon the cross forgave
Perhaps we can forgive each other too?

"I think, therefore I am."
Cogito, ergo sum
Is it possible to be more than
We think we must become?

Sentio, ergo sum
"I feel, therefore I am"
In my heart, I do hold hope
Someday maybe we can.

HINDSIGHT IS BUT(t) A SPHINCTER

the world today is bullshit
and you know it.
take it from a poet.
not me, necessarily,
but read some poetry
and you will see
what I mean:

pure, capital BS
bullshit!

or, let's just continue to
cycle through
the "news"
24 hours
a
day
even as we
try
to
dream
and act as if this is all
somehow
something new—
"who knew?"
like we haven't
already
seen this bullshit
1000 times before…

10,000 times to be sure!

ad infinitum:

black hat.

white hat.

BROWN hat.

nothing new
under the sun;
just a steaming,
heaping pile
of festering bullshit
getting hotter
every year.

you know what they say: you can't polish a turd, but you can...

QUESTION SHIT

I have often wondered if,
at the tolling of the bell,
While perched on gilded
porcelain thrones
Will the filthy rich shit well?

When Horsemen ride black skies
And Amber Waves are turned to ashes
Will they still clutch tightly
to their pearls
Or will they fall out of their asses?

With judgement handed down
As that final check comes due
Will the customary tip be left? Or
merely smears of fear
and wet doodoo?

Oh, how the filthy rich shit well today!
A fecal reign from up on high
How do they digest the thought
That, rich or poor, we all must die?

I contemplate these things
Along with my hypocrisies - -
If given half a chance, might I
     not also shit on me?

PAM

You called everybody "Babe."
Loved animals, your late husband
& sweet Mary Jane.
You made a hell of a good pot roast
& would always let me borrow your car
during my lunch breaks
for reasons you'd have rather not known about
and never did bother to ask.
(Let's just say I could make the Kessel Run
in under 12 parsecs back then and leave it at that.)
You were a no bullshit New Jersey gal
with a heart of gold—but woe to all that voted conservative!—
and I'll cherish those old times together
in your little house off Shade
'neath a blanket of smoke
where your door was always open
to the wayward

of which
I was one.

BUSTA'

ATTENTION

Whole Foods shoppers and Employees,

Today is a bittersweet day in the prepared foods section of our store
For today, we lose one of our very best:

A devoted father
A Pirate
A Raider
A Champion
and a true friend.

The Man Who Is To SHEER GUTS
What Frank Sinatra Was To Musical Talent—

The one,
Thee only,

Mr. Joe
Bustamante.

So come on by and say goodbye, because I gotta go

Those... uhhh... "Guys" are looking for me.

You know...

"Doze Guyz"

MIRROR

beauty's
vanity

perfection's
insanity

definies me
defies me

denies me
my peace

as i
reach for

the makeup
the scissor
the blade

lie's ideal
false idols
life idled away

slave to some
unspoken urge
to obey

duck face
selfie
hashtagfire
i'll see you
all
in hell.

CHINESE FOOD

at the end of the indulgence
came a styrofoam cookie,
capper to the whole sordid affair,
with my fortune
which read:

"Your first and last love is self love"

ah...

how
touching—
quite literally

as well as prophetic,
dear reader,

that i would happen to be touching myself
right now.

Lucky Numbers:

12, 14, 18, 13! 24, 28

SHIPMATES

Private Pirate Friendships
Ships in the night
A port from the storm
So wrong that it's right

Pure Pirate Friendships
Docked in real tight
Wicks burning at both ends
Flaming so bright

Salty sea captain
Greenhorn first mate
Splintered wet pegleg
Stands rigid and straight

"Shiver me timbers!
All hands on deck!
We're chasing that White Whale—
Boys, we'll take what we get!"

Ishmael and Ahab
And cabin boy Pip
Never seen nothin'
Like Ol' Moby Dick

Tashtego The Gay Head
Under Queequeg's harpoon
Glistens in seafoam
Neath nautical moon

Poop Deck Pirate Friendships
Hot Pequod nights
The squall of a fierce storm
So wrong, yet so right

Proud Pirate Friendships
Seagulls take flight
Off the coast of Nantucket
A rainbow of light!

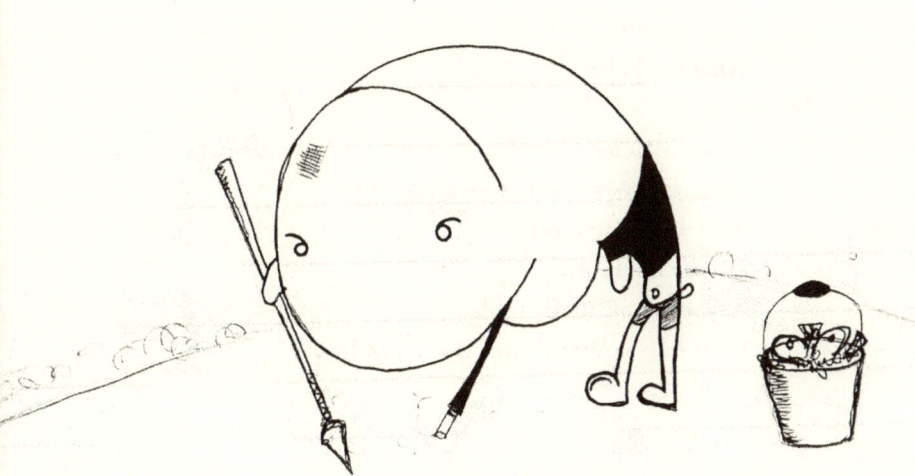

TALL TALE FROM A SHALLOW GUTTER

Tall was the tale
And shallow the gutter
Many an evening
Spent fooling each other
The horror of morning
Eyelids like steel shutters
Could not feel my goddamn legs

But, oh what great lies we would tell!
And how we put up with the smell
Of mop bucket sweat
Man, I'll make you a bet
That this story ain't gonna end well

Fuck it, tho,
bro, ya know?
What the hell?

Cabana Memories
Of weekdays at the Powerhouse
Arm wrestling mini-Mr. T
I'd pity the fools
Never fell off their stools
What sad, sanitized lives they must lead

Romantic notions of not being a complete louse
Rather, King Of Dive Bar Karaoke
Through Long Island drool,
I always played it so cool
Singing: "The piano has been drinking, not me."

"Remember that time?"
Ha! How could I forget?
Christ we sure were three sheets
Bone soaked through

"Remember her name?"
Nah, man, crap I forget.
Only vaguely recall some
half-hearted "I love you's."
Nothin' too real to grasp onto

When I said that I loved her
Heck, that was all just pretext
For one more tall tale from the gutter
Bartender, I'll have me another

But oh what great lines we would tell!
And how we would cast our spells
Now I wish we never met
As I cash in my bet
This story sure turned out unwell.

The pissing turtle TOAD

TOO STONED TO SLOW DANCE
with Bryan Daniel Peffley
(for Mikey)

I'm too stoned to slow dance
I'm too dulled for romance
A half enough is bad enough as it is
And I've been lulled into thinkin'
That the answer's keep drinkin'
What else is new
beneath the tropicali sun?
Nothin' new
under a tropical setting sun

Like that last lonely hotdog
left cold on the grill
Like a mangy old lost dog
alone on a hill
Like a case of craft brew
When all you drink is the swill
Forever confused
and never no fun
I'll pay my bill when I'm goddamn
Good and done

And it's woe, woe is me
Why's it always gotta me be?
Where's the Job Johnny on this island?
I've gotta take a leak

And it's what, what could be?
Could've been maybe,
but I'll never see
Just let me drain my lizard in peace.

ONE MONTH CHIP

Little bit manic,
anxious,
that Summer feeling
of cold rosé
creeping up my spine
trying to infect my brain stem.
Thunderstorms and
hangovers
on the horizon...
Swimming pools filled
with soda water,
citrus spritz, and STRONG spirit.
Cheap blow-up raft from K-Mart
to try and keep myself afloat.

Tequila was last July's muse
through most of September.
I always switch to beer in the Fall:
Pumpkin, Stout, Guinness with Rum–
Yo ho Ho! Ho! Ho!
"Merry vodka straight in three finger pours—
Happy Butt Yeast!"

Does Sober January really count
if you're just counting down the days until
Piss In The Fridge February
comes along?
All of those locally grown
organic bell peppers...
buoyant in the crisper drawer.
And me, steadily sinking to the bottom
on an installment plan.

Yes, it's been many a long Winter.

But no sense dwelling in the past
when we've all this present to unwrap.

It's Springtime in my
heart
as I hand-roll a
cigarette
in the part of my mind
that still wishes he were
"Chocolat" era
Johnny Depp
or some-fucking-body
while
"Hi, my name is Eric,
and I'm an alcoholic."
shoves an
un-micturated-upon
carrot stick
between his
big
dumb
grinning
sober lips.

EVER

never
trust
a
junkie
who
doesn't
smoke.

"JAM UP!"

you haven't died
until you've worked in a
frozen fundraiser pizza plant
in Central Pennsylvania
in the dead of winter
while in withdrawal
with your asshole buddy Phil,
who just cut his hair into
"Exile" era Keith Richards bangs
in the bathroom
on his lunch break,
mopping the floor with aplomb
as if anyone could be
that into mopping
(or those bangs for that matter)
if they hadn't scored some
Wiz-Mac bags from LaTroy
on the sly earlier that morning
in the cheese cooler—
so much for our supposed
"solidarity in suffering"
—but we lived
and we died alone
in times like those, when
"Jam Up And Jelly Tight"
    by Tommy Roe
came on the oldies station
just in time for the stromboli wrapper
to grind to a halt
for the 5th time that day
while Phil,
dancing a sweaty jig now,
sang along
into his mop handle.

THE ALGORITHM OF "IZ"
(for the brothers Nort)

The redundancy of "IZ"
Is in harmony with
The algorithm of IZness

For instance:
"Iz iz?" the question
Can be answered by
"Iz." "Iz iz." or "Iz iz, iz."

"But how can this IZ?"
You may ask
Answered simply:
"Be iz." "Iz be iz." or only
    with one lonely "IZ."

"Iz iz Be iz?"
Exactly!
Now you're catching on, iz
Or more plainly put:
"Now you IZin', you Iz."

Not to be confused
With you IZ'n, as in:
"Be Iz not Iz," or
"No be Iz, Iz Iz."

Simple, right?

Now let's pretend you want to
Express approval:
"That's Iz!"
Or you can drop
"that is" completely
And again be just "IZ!"

Isn't Iz Iz?
Well iz sho' nuff IZ
Even when iz ain't even
Iz often times Iz...

Be Iz that iz!

Iz be do Iz iz too!
All the time—
Everyday—Iz iz iz—
Iz Be Do!

Damn Iz be coo!
Be Iz do Iz, iz true!!!

Now you try it IZ!
Go on! Give Iz an Iz.
Iz be only iz as iz
You think Iz be iz.

— IT'S ONLY A SIGN OF INSANITY
       IF YOU DON'T OWN A DOG —

LAST NIGHT, 'ROUND 3AM
FOR NO GOOD REASON AT ALL
I FELT LIKE SITTING ON
THE ~~KIT~~ KITCHEN FLOOR
IN MY UNDERWEAR
NEXT TO THE DOG FOOD
AND HAVING A WARM BEER
AND A HAND ROLLED SMOKE

SO I DID
AND IT WAS GOOD

GUESS THAT'S 'BOUT REASON ENOUGH

MASON JAR MEMORIES

Remember this when
Moonlight sits low in your window
Like "One Last Shot"
Of romanticized shine:

Those were not the days.

MOTHER MOLLOY

from the shadows
outside Video Renaissance
she emerged,
Moses staff in hand

as classical music seemed to
swell behind a night's sky

where Golden Apple
dinner théâtre ghosts
and Bee Ridge
dive bar piss-oleros
raised sewing thimble toasts
to bills unpaid
and the beauty of
Ravel's Boléro.

MY DOG IS NOT A CAT PERSON

My dog is not a cat person
My dog is not a person
But if he were, he'd be a people person
Of that I am quite certain

My dog has never met a person
For whom he did not have affection
But if he did, he'd know he could rely
On this good boy for his protection

Yes, I am my dog's good boy
And he is my good boy too
I hope someday you may find a friend
Who means as much to you

Perhaps your friend will be feline
If so, please know i wouldn't mind
Still, I feel I speak for my canine
When I say that he is not the feline kind.

A WIFE'S LAMENT

Enough of this

GODDESS

"Diva Cup"

Claptrap!

Like we've got the ghost
Of Whitney Houston herself
shoved up our yoni holes—

"GOOP, there it is!"

Flooding the crimson
outhouse toilets
As we Spirit-Weave a tapestry
that mere-mortal-man
can never possibly
understand.

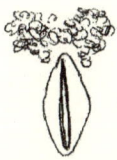

THE DILETTANTE AND THE RENAISSANCE MAN

eating some
apricot sherbet
that Jenna made
(sugar free /
dairy free, of course)
when it occurs to me
that I
am merely
a
dilettante,
while my wife
is
a Renaissance Man.

THEM!

BEWARE
all
those
whose
capacity
for outrage
far exceeds
the very narrow
limits of
their own
stagnating
imaginations.

EXPRESSION OF GOD

Old black homeless man dancing
conducting early morning traffic
laughing at some silent joke
he alone appears to hear
that sure seems to be
on the rest of us
as our cars
congest
slowly
down
La
B
r
e
a.

PRESSURE

everything I have ever done
in my entire life
has led up
to THIS

but I suppose
the same could be said
about taking my next piss
should I be **#blessed** enough
to make it
to THAT point

...

ahhhhhhhhhhhh
sweet relief.

OUTPOURING OF LIKE

I want to thank you in advance,
friends, for the outpouring of Like
I'll be feeling so much better
With a warm dopamine spike

And I won't need drugs or alcohol
To lift myself out of this rut
While basking in the instant validation
Of double digit blue thumbs up

So please don't mindlessly scroll by
And throw this man in need a bone
Meantime, I'll just be sitting here
Blankly staring at my phone.

EUROPE PLAYLIST

I walked through the streets of Soho in the rain
but Lee Ho Fook's was closed for good.
There would be no beef chow mein, and
although my hair was far from perfect
I let out a howl anyway.

I saw a crowd of young London Boys
foolin' around in the corner, drunk and dressed
in their best fashions of the day.
I envied their youth, while at the same time admiring
my early-middle-aged late blooming sobriety
& timeless sense of personal style.

I crossed the street at Abbey Road
with the rest of the tourists, despite
The Beatles conspicuous absence from
this playlist (Señor Coconut, anyone?).
They will forever be the most fab.

And whether enjoying a plate of Fish & Chips
at the famed Champion's Pub where Freddy Mercury
so iconically wrote, or experiencing the sublime wonder
that is Proper English High Tea, it turns out Roger Miller
was right: EN-GL-AND really does swing like a pendulum do.

We felt the city's call while on a long walk
along the roiling River Thames as I never felt so much
alike.

        alike.

                alike.

Later on
in the City of Light
we took a waltz at midnight
with the spirits of the old masters
beneath a starry, starry night's sky,
with it's impressionistic palette of beautiful
blues and greys. And in the morning

sat together in a park in Paris, France
reading the news, which, I'm sorry to report,
still looks pretty bad even after all these years.
Seems like they just won't give peace a chance no how
(no matter how many times we say it).

    Rest In Peace Jim Morrison ~
    LONGUE VIE Shane MacGowan!

I came looking for answers and I guess you could say
I found a few, along with a couple of questions I hadn't
even thought to think of yet (boy I sure hope Pearl & Roy
made it in the end, those crazy kids). And tho some of it's magic,
and some of it's tragic, all and all I'm feeling quite transcendent
and relaxed, thank you very much. Now—"Laissez-Moi Tranquille!"

California, I'm comin' home.

ASSPOCI LA BUTTE

Asspoci La Butte
Wears a green TamBéret
He quit drinkin' wine
Now whines about it and brays

Just one Gauloises
At a Paris café
And one more, and one more,
And one more, S'il vous plaît

Asspoci La Butte
Is an artist by trade
And tho he ain't no Picasso
He's well on his way

"His work is quite phallic"
Euro art critics say
It would look so well hung
In some Swiss miss's chalet

Oh Oh Asspoci
The "C" is pronounced like a "K"
Oh Oh Asspoci
I'd plant a flag in your hill anyday

Asspoci's been known
To dabble in clay
And erect "dome-like-structures"
Out of papier-mâché

He paints with his fingers
Like he's in the third grade
"Jesus hates it when you smoke"
Is written on his ashtray

Monsieur La Butte
Does not walk, he sashays
Has a harem of groupies
All under his sway

Along with his own
Personal attaché
To source his sardines
And work weeks without pay

Oh Oh Asspoci
Don't throw your genius away
Oh Oh Asspoci
You'll get your due due someday

Asspoci La Butte
Never orders gourmet
He's completely content
With a Haddock fillet

Against the bourgeois
Indignantly he inveighs
His next show's set to open
Off off off Broadway

Philistines find
La Butte's style too cliché
But this never causes
Asspoci dismay

Baguette in his pocket
Mood merry and gay
He may well be the gayest
This side of Marseille!

Oh Oh Asspoci
You were not born to obey
Oh Oh Asspoci
Your soul must be put on display ~

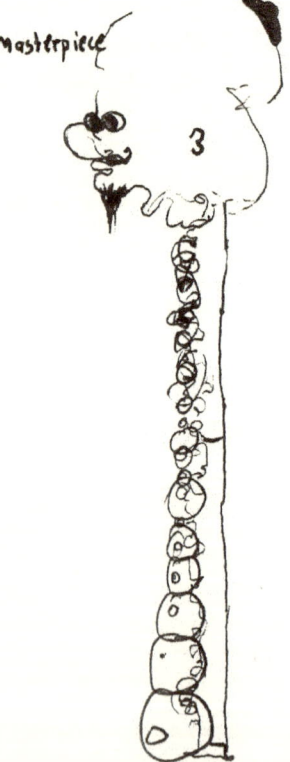

PARLEZ VOUS JE T'AIME
Midnight in Paris, 2/19/2020
(pour Jenna)

Pardon me
Ma Chérie
But I must ask again
Parlez vous "Je t'aime"

Excusez-moi
Ooh la la
Oui, je le parle. Et vous?
Do you speak, "I love you?"

Yes, I do too—
Oui, je le parle aussi!
Won't you speak
Just a little with me?

Yes! Yes!
Mon Amour

Oui! Oui!
My Love—
Oui!

Je T'aime
Mon Amour…

Ça Suffit!

THE TAO OF GRANDPA ROMAN

"every morning
i get up
take a look at myself
in the mirror
& think
thank god
that ugly sonovabitch
isn't me!"

SELF LOVE
(for N. Smikey)

I,
Oh hi.
There you are.
I love you so!
Just thought you should know.
Each morning my love grows.
It wasn't always like this.
Days past I shunned my reflection;
Hazy eyes blurred by shame and regret.
Now, when these eyes meet my own, we both smile.

NOSTALGIA (PART 2)

Tiny ember glories
Always make the finest stories
Nostalgia is the only thing
I can recall
Label me romantic
Call me the flip side of pedantic
Broad strokes are more appealing
After all

The Devil's in the details
God is in the gist
There's a gale up in the topsail
The mills overflow with grist
If it's not remembered fondly
Friends, I say it won't be missed
Ain't got no time for ennui, darlin'
I still can taste your kiss

Rock me to sleep so gently
With a lullaby of youth
Embellish all you want to
I didn't come here for the truth

And lay me down so easy
In the grass of my hometown
Lead my mind down hallowed pathways
Where as kids we ran around

Fireflies of summer
Light up like lanterns along the way
To the blazing backyard bonfire
Kindled dreams of yesterday

Here I'll stay.

PICTURE OF THREE

A picture of three heads
Snuggled in bed
A picture of three kids
After prayers have been said
A picture of three,
Pretty soon to be four
They say a picture's worth a thousand words
I say it's worth more

Dear Sweet Jesus thank you
For all that we have
Bless Bryan & Caitlin
Jess, Me, Mom & Dad

And help us hang on
Through the maudlin and mad
Let us laugh with each other
Comfort us when we're sad

And help us hold on
Make us graceful and glad
Always grateful and gracious
Gallant as Galahad

And Lord let us dream
Them childhood dreams
Keep us from sinnin' too bad

Forever tethered together
Though time may pull us apart
Bound down deep in our hearts
~
For worse or for better
I loved you right from the start
Crowned down deep in my heart

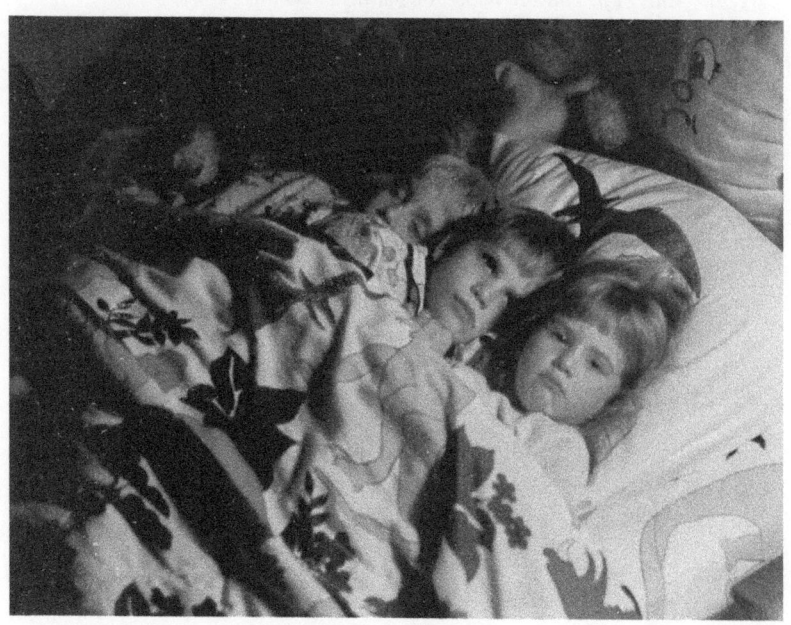

GOLDEN ASHES
(a poem by my mother, Izabella Maria Peffley, 1980)

A second chance at love lost,
Resurrecting longings buried beneath duties and predictability

A heart again alive with youthful anticipation,
Needing only your voice to make it a gentle world once more

Wishing to impart to you laughter, wonder, and passion,
Receiving in return promises that soar me toward belief in impossibilities

You became for me what my dreams used to be,
Lingering sighs, entwined hopes, porch swings in moonlight by the ocean

*Sometimes the first love is the truest - the most honest measure
of who we are, and all we might become,
A piece of the puzzle that fits so effortlessly into the core of our souls*

*But the years which passed proved too many,
The layers of reality and responsibility too deep to eclipse*

*Nonetheless, the love will remain until the final sunset,
My wish for a kind life for you continues undiminished*

*A second chance at love lost,
My treasured path in recapturing the timeless quality
of a heart profoundly in love with you*

SIMPLY
(a poem by my father)

There is something in the air,
After a rain.
The sky so gray.
The earth so wet.
There is something in me,
After a rain.
The wonderfulness of being:
Being of Life,
Being of Love,
Being of Peace,
Simply Being!

ABP 1974

we

the world
would be
a
markedly better place
if everyday
WE
read
and tried ourselves
to write
a little bit
of
poetry.

ESP 20/20

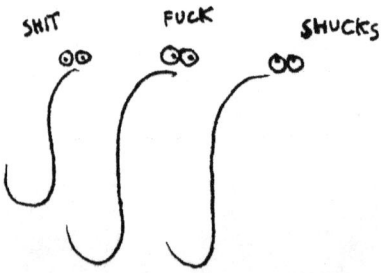

**END
S
P**

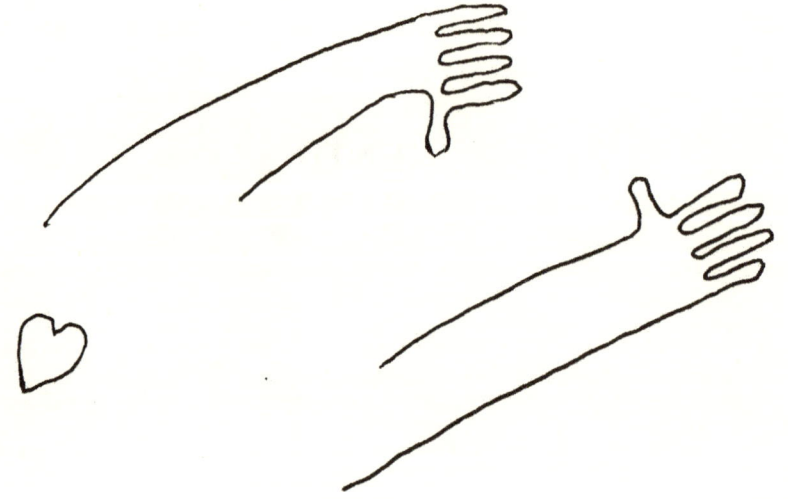

and to J bird, the best wife,
friend, beautiful gal
I'm fortunate
to share my life with ~

ERIC STEPHEN PEFFLEY is the author of the previous poetry collections *"Songs In Search of Music / The Rip-Off Poems"* and *"Me, In the Membership of My Days."* He lives in Los Angeles with his wife and creative partner Jenna Ohnemus Peffley and their beloved dog, Bubbs. Now that this collection is complete, he's working on taking it a day at a time. And while he is not a psychic, he does play one on TV.

{question shit}

$15.00
ISBN 978-0-578-66856-7
51500>

www.ingramcontent.com/pod-product-compliance
Lightning Source LLC
Chambersburg PA
CBHW020947090426
42736CB00010B/1303